W9-CCD-282

FAMOUS PEOPLE

Steve
Irwin

by P.M. Boekhoff and
Stuart A. Kallen

**KIDHAVEN
PRESS™**

THOMSON
™
GALE

San Diego • Detroit • New York • San Francisco • Cleveland
New Haven, Conn. • Waterville, Maine • London • Munich

© 2004 by KidHaven Press. KidHaven Press is an imprint of The Gale Group, Inc., a division of Thomson Learning, Inc.

KidHaven™ and Thomson Learning™ are trademarks used herein under license.

For more information, contact
KidHaven Press
27500 Drake Rd.
Farmington Hills, MI 48331-3535
Or you can visit our Internet site at http://www.gale.com

LIBRARY OF CONGRESS CATALOGING-IN-PUBLICATION DATA

Boekhoff, P.M. (Patti Marlene), 1957–
  Steve Irwin / by P.M. Boekhoff and Stuart A. Kallen.
    p. cm.—(Famous people)
Summary: Profiles Steve Irwin, a herpetologist, television personality, and movie star whose concern for the natural environment and animals led him to fame as the "Crocodile Hunter."
Includes bibliographical references and index.
  ISBN 0-7377-1890-0 (hardback : alk. paper)
   1. Irwin, Steve—Juvenile literature. 2. Herpetologists—Australia—Biography—Juvenile literature. [1. Irwin, Steve. 2. Herpetologists. 3. Television personalities. 4. Scientists.]
I. Kallen, Stuart A., 1955– II. Title. III. Series.
  QL31.I78B64 2004
  597.9'092—dc22

                                                          2003013326

Printed in the United States of America

CONTENTS

CHAPTER ONE

Wild Child

Steve Irwin is a crocodile hunter, a **reptile** expert, and a TV and movie star. He is also an environmentalist—someone who works to protect the natural environment from destruction or pollution. While Irwin is a big star today and known to millions of fans, he has shown his love for animals since he was very young. And even as a little boy he was always taking risks by handling dangerous wildlife.

Stephen Robert Irwin was born in Victoria, Australia, on February 22, 1962. His mother, Lynn, was a maternity nurse who also worked to help sick and orphaned animals. His father, Bob, was a plumber who loved the remote, wild lands of Australia known as the bush. Many unique species of reptiles that can be found only in Australia live in this wilderness.

Steve was a wild child who liked to go fishing and hunting for reptiles. On Steve's sixth birthday, his mom and dad gave him the present he always wanted: a snake big enough to eat him! Although Steve was too small to play with his twelve-foot-long scrub python, he loved the snake and named him Fred. In order to feed his new pet, Steve went out several times a week to catch fish and hunt rodents.

Fred was the start of an animal collection that would grow into a zoo. Over the next two years, Steve and his father collected dozens of snakes and lizards.

Steve Irwin comes face to face with a hungry crocodile. Steve has been handling dangerous wildlife since he was a child.

"I remember my dad . . . catching highly **venomous** snakes, with nothing more than his bare hands and sharp reflexes," said Steve. "I used to watch in an [excited] stare, as my dad captured . . . the most venomous snakes in the world."[1]

The Deadly Brown Snake

As they searched for reptiles among the boulders and bushes, Steve liked to pretend he was in the army and his father was the enemy. One day when Steve was seven, he ran ahead of his father, climbed up some boulders, and aimed his stick in the direction from which he expected his father to appear. Then he noticed a seven-foot-long brown snake flicking its tongue on his foot.

Steve knew that the snake was smelling him with special glands on his tongue to find out whether he could eat Steve, or whether Steve might eat him. Steve also knew it was the second-most-venomous snake in the world and it could kill him, but he had no fear. He put his foot down on the middle of the snake's body, pinning it down so it could not escape. The angry snake hissed while Steve proudly shouted to his dad. He had caught a big brown snake all by himself!

When Mr. Irwin realized that Steve was toying with an extremely poisonous snake, he ran over and knocked his son into the air to move him quickly away from the reptile. Steve came crashing down on the rocks, in terrible pain. His proud moment turned to confusion as his father shouted at him and called him an idiot.

Steve handles a big snake. He has years of experience handling poisonous reptiles.

Steve ran away crying until he ran out of breath. He decided to run away from home and live in a cave forever. Seeing a huge crack in some rocks, he peeked inside to see if it was a cave he could live in. But there was already a family of beautiful lizards living in the cave. Steve recognized them as Cunninghams skinks, and he spent the rest of the day trying to coax them out with blades of grass. When the sky began to get dark Steve heard the sound of his dad's car horn and

Duck hunters camp by the side of a lake near Victoria, Australia. As a young boy, Steve liked to fish and hunt for reptiles in the area around Victoria.

said good-bye to his lizard friends, his plans for running away forgotten.

The Lesson

Steve rode home in silence, knowing his father was angry. Even at seven, Steve knew better than to put his own life in danger. His father probably saved his life that day, but Steve would still get a chance to study the snake. After Steve ran away, Mr. Irwin caught the deadly creature and brought it home for their collection.

Although he had a close call, Steve never gave up trying to catch poisonous snakes. Later, when he was bored at a ball game with some other boys, Steve filled an entire cooler with venomous snakes he caught by their tails. The other boys were very impressed at his daring, but his father was not. This time, Steve got in trouble for endangering the lives of the other kids. To Steve, it always seemed like he was in trouble, but he later realized his father's lessons taught him not to endanger his own life or the lives of others.

Beerwah

Steve and his father continued to collect reptiles until the Irwin house was overflowing with slithering, poisonous creatures. In 1970 the Irwins solved this problem by moving to Queensland to start a small reptile park at Beerwah on what is called Australia's Sunshine Coast. Over the next three years, Steve worked in the park with his dad, building homes for the animals that closely resembled their natural **habitats**.

On their family reptile farm, Steve helped his mother raise orphaned kangaroos.

Living in a reptile park was a dream come true for Steve, and there were always many enjoyable jobs to perform. Steve worked with his mother to raise orphaned kangaroos, wallabies, koalas, and wombats. When they were old enough to be on their own, Steve and his mom released those animals back into their natural habitats.

Steve went with his dad on field trips for weeks at a time, catching snakes, lizards, and crocodiles for their zoo. Steve described the desert **outback** experience: "From scorchingly unbearable heat to freezing cold. . . . When the dust storms pass, you've got to handle . . . having a swarm of writhing flies all over your body from sunup to sundown."[2]

Jumping Crocs

Steve and his dad shared many such adventures. When Steve was nine, he went along with his dad to rescue some freshwater crocodiles whose water hole was going to be drained and filled in. Each night Steve steered the boat and shined a bright spotlight into the shining eyes of the crocodiles, which caused them to stay still.

When the boat drifted close to the stunned crocodile, Steve's dad jumped on its back and wrestled it into the boat. Young Steve then took control of the crocodile by jumping on its back and holding on tight. The crocodile would thrash him against the sides of the boat until his dad jumped in and put the animal in a bag.

One night Steve's dad took the spotlight and told him to go to the front of the boat, the position for jumping onto a crocodile! Steve could see the crocodile's teeth shining in the dark as he waited for exactly the right moment to pounce. At his father's command, he slammed onto the croc's bony back with his fingers wrapped around the reptile's long neck and his legs wrapped around the tail. The crocodile was as big as Steve!

Steve was thrashed in the muddy water as the crocodile pulled him down to the bottom of the hole. He held on while the crocodile rolled underwater and

Steve subdues a ferocious crocodile. Steve has tamed many crocodiles since he wrestled his first one as a boy.

tried to bite him. Soon his father's arm felt them under the murky water, caught them both, and slammed them into the boat. It was a proud moment for father and son, and the beginning of Steve's long career as a crocodile hunter.

Fear and Love

Steve Irwin had been handling snakes and other dangerous animals at the Beerwah Reptile Park from the time he was eight years old. Throughout his childhood and teen years, Steve came to love and respect the animals and, in fact, thought of them as his brothers and sisters. By 1980, the Irwin family zoo included more than 150 crocodiles and had been renamed the Queensland Reptile and Fauna Park.

In the early 1980s, Steve's dad told him he had decided to rescue some of the biggest, most dangerous saltwater crocodiles in the world and make a home for them in their park. These crocodiles had reputations as evil, ugly monsters waiting to kill people. Although they were just as important to Australia's ecosystem as other animals, they were endangered by frightened fishermen and farmers who shot at them.

Steve and his dad went out to look for the crocodiles; then Steve was often left to trap them by himself

Steve laid the groundwork for his television show early on by videotaping himself catching crocodiles.

while his dad went back home to take care of the zoo. Steve set out on his dangerous missions with his dog Sui and a video camera. When catching the big crocs, Steve tied the camera to a tree or stuck it in the mud.

When he came home after a successful three-month crocodile hunt, Steve liked to go surfing with his buddies. By taking videos of his captures, he was able to prove to them that while he was gone he was out catching crocodiles with his bare hands.

During his hunting trips, Steve spent a lot of time alone out in the mangroves. Steve fished for his food and squatted barefoot among the buzzing mosquitoes and other insects for hours at a time. To find relief from the insects—and hide from the wily crocodiles—he covered himself with leaves and mud.

Sometimes he felt overwhelmed by the awesome responsibility he faced alone. Steve said:

> I probably don't show fear, but I suffer from fear like everyone else. You know, there's a fear aspect for me that happens all the time. . . . And that's what keeps me at a safe distance. Because when [crocodiles] strike it can be that quick that if they're within range, you're dead, you're dead in your tracks. And his head weighs more than my body so it's WHACK! . . . and I'd just blow up. It's that powerful.[3]

Catching Agro

As careful as he was, sometimes the crocodiles were able to wound Steve. One day he wrestled with a crocodile in the water, dragged it to shore, and heaved the croc up onto the mud. During the entire struggle, the crocodile had four of Steve's fingers in his mouth.

Steve dragged the struggling beast to his truck, ripped off the seat cover with his own teeth, and blindfolded the animal, which calmed it down. Then he finally got his bloody fingers out of the reptile's giant jaws and saw the large gash he had gotten on his face. Instead of going to the hospital, Steve bandaged his wounds and rested so he could catch another crocodile the next day.

The next morning Steve went out not knowing that he was about to meet one of the meanest crocodiles in the world. When he approached his crocodile net in his boat, it was underwater, and the trapped reptile was thrashing fiercely. As Steve drew the net closer to his boat, the giant crocodile angrily smashed against the boat. When Steve got the croc's tail into the boat, it pivoted on its tail and lunged to eat him. Because this animal was causing him so much aggravation, Steve named him Agro.

An enormous crocodile lunges at Steve with gaping jaws.

Steve grabbed Agro's tail and heaved the crocodile into the boat as he jumped into the water with his dog under his arm. "Holy Snappin' duck poo!,"[4] Steve gurgled in the water. Agro head butted the boat so hard he split the aluminum, and water poured in. On his way back, Steve went ashore twice to bail out the boat. After catching Agro, Steve went to the hospital to get his hand stitched up and the new gash in his face tended to.

Agro the Educator

Agro has never forgiven Steve for catching him. He hates Steve, and whenever he sees Steve at the park, he tries to crush Steve in half and eat him. Many times he has chased Steve away and then attacked the tools and clothes Steve left behind during his quick escapes. Agro has ripped apart two lawn mowers, a shovel, brush cutters, and a hat and shoe after chasing Steve out of his territory. Steve calls Agro a beautiful but naughty croc.

Steve and Agro perform for a crowd of people every day at the zoo. And every day Agro shows the visitors to the park just how a crocodile protects his territory. He hides in ambush, then strikes out at Steve with lightning speed, educating people about the dangers of this often hidden predator.

Meeting Terri Raines

One day in October 1992, Steve and Agro were giving their demonstration in the park. Terri Raines, a young American woman from Oregon, was visiting

Steve and his assistants move Agro from his pen at the Australia Zoo.

for the first time. Terri was amazed at how calm Steve looked as he held out a chicken and the giant crocodile snapped it up into his powerful jaws. Steve was amazed by Terri, too:

> I met my wife Terri while I was doing one of my routine crocodile demonstrations at Australia Zoo. And would you believe it—I'm in there and I'm trying to stay alive 'cuz Agro, this big

Steve and Terri pose with a baby kangaroo. Steve met Terri as he was performing with Agro and it was love at first sight.

crocodile, he's trying to kill me. And I looked up into the crowd and I saw this woman. Our eyes met, my heart started thumping and it was love at first sight.[5]

After the demonstration, Steve and Terri began to talk and soon became lost in conversation. And the two shared something in common: Back home in Oregon, Terri restored injured predators such as foxes, possums, raccoons, bears, bobcats, and cougars and released them back into the wild. She was looking for a zoo that would take some of her cougars. Terri said:

When Steve and I met we were talking about how much we love animals that kill with their teeth, and it was so romantic because Steve loves crocodiles and I love cougars, and they both kill with their teeth and isn't that wild. And then we were talking about how we don't do birds very well, because we are both deathly afraid of parrots. Imagine how romantic that was. Steve said, parrots always bite me on the nose. I said they always get my ear. It was fabulous.[6]

The couple had many adventures together as they got to know one another. They visited each other and planned to get married. Soon Steve and Terri would have incredible daring adventures together. They would depend upon each other in life-and-death situations. And they would capture their adventures on film, sharing their amazing experiences with the world.

CHAPTER THREE

The Crocodile Hunter

Steve Irwin spent many years alone catching crocodiles in the bush, but his life changed forever when he married Terri Raines on June 4, 1992. And although he had been bitten by snakes and nearly eaten by crocodiles, Steve said getting married was the scariest moment of his life! Steve was so nervous that he was shaking and sweating and he felt his tie was strangling him like a python. In fact, Steve said he would rather face a giant crocodile!

It was not long before he got his wish. While on their honeymoon, Steve and Terri began filming their first television documentary, *The Crocodile Hunter, Part 1*. In the film, Steve got a call to catch a crocodile in a mosquito-infested swamp and Terri agreed to go along. They camped in a tent, and when Terri went out in the morning she was scared by a snake. It was

In a scene from the movie The Crocodile Hunter: Collision Course, *a crocodile slams into Steve and Terri's boat.*

scared too, and it reared up and hissed at her! She yelled for Steve, and he came out and caught the poisonous red-bellied black snake.

The couple's adventures continued when they were filming *The Crocodile Hunter, Part 2*. On that shoot, after baiting a croc trap with a wild pig, Terri and Sui fell overboard. As he helped them out of the crocodile-infested water, Steve was bitten repeatedly by a python. They finally netted a crocodile and got it out of the trap, but Terri was terrified as Steve instructed her to climb on top of the reptile and hold it down.

The crocodile was scared and nervous too, and they covered the animal's eyes to calm it down. Then Steve jumped on the crocodile and rode it down to the boat. Terri said it was the most awesome experience of her life. And the situation helped the couple learn to work together and count on each other in life-and-death situations as they were being filmed by their friend John Stainton.

"By Crikey!"

When *The Crocodile Hunter* was shown on television, it became a huge success. Over the next three years, Steve made ten one-hour episodes that were seen by 500 million people all over the world. The show features Steve, bleeding and covered with mud, thrashing around with crocodiles and wrestling with them until they are tired. Despite his pain or fear, Steve never loses his sense of humor. After a dragged-out fight with a croc, he will say to the camera, "Isn't she a

Steve calms a crocodile by covering its eyes and holding it tightly as Terri guides their boat.

beauty?" Other times he coos "hello, sweetheart" to a 330-pound python coiled neatly around his neck.

With the popularity of the show, Steve became known for his outback slang, using words such as *by crikey* (wow), *bloke* (man), *sheila* (woman), *G'day, mate* (good day, friend), and *Oz* (Australia).

Despite his success and fame, Steve still wears his Australian bush-trekker khaki shorts and shirt and thick leather boots everywhere he goes. In one documentary, he wore his khakis and boots underwater to feed hungry sharks from a shark cage. He even wore the outfit to a fancy party in New York, with Terri dressed in an elegant dress.

In the outback, Steve's thick leather boots help to keep him from getting bitten by snakes, insects, and other creatures. Steve nearly lost one of his boots, however, along with his life, when a raging, flesh-eating Komodo dragon bit his heel as he scrambled up a tree to get away. The Komodo dragon's spit is deadly poison, and the thick leather boot probably saved Steve's life.

Up Close

Steve puts himself in all kinds of danger by getting extremely close to some of nature's fiercest creatures. He gets very close to the camera, too, so his extreme enthusiasm is right in the audience's face. And Terri said this behavior never stops: "[He's] like this 24 hours a day, 7 days a week. I don't really work with him, I just kind of keep up with him. And it is an exciting lifestyle. Every day is an adventure, and you never know what's around the next corner. I just love it."[7]

In his high-energy dramas, Steve says he has been "peed on, pooed on, stomped on, bitten, chomped, sliced, chased, harassed—by animals, mate."[8] Says *TV Guide* senior critic Matt Roush. "He doesn't just handle animals. He is handled by animals, and somehow escapes with his skin."[9]

While Steve's show is exciting, it also teaches a lesson. Since its 1996 debut, *Crocodile Hunter* has inspired young people to care about the world's endangered species. Fans say this is because Steve looks at the world from the animal's point of view, trying to understand how the animal feels and what is in its best interest.

Insanely Dangerous

Many of the things Steve does, however, seem insanely dangerous. About once a week Terri is afraid for her life, or for Steve's. And sometimes Steve has to jump in and save her life, so the show is always very exciting. Steve takes responsibility for the lives of everyone who works with him to make sure everyone survives while making the *Crocodile Hunter* documentaries.

In life-and-death situations, Steve and his coworkers depend on each other. Tragically, sometimes Steve cannot completely prevent terrible accidents. For example, while Steve was working with his best friend, Wes Mannion, the director of the Australia Zoo, Graham the crocodile attacked Wes and tore two huge chunks out of his leg. Graham was about to eat Wes's head when Steve stepped in:

> If that [crocodile] had bit his head, it just would have popped it, so I . . . twisted the croc up like that so the crocodile then swung around to try and kill me, which gave Wes enough time to get up on the fence. Here's the beauty, though. When Wes got up on the fence he turned— blood's pumping out, he's missing two big

With his face inches from its powerful jaws, Steve subdues a crocodile. Crocodile hunting is extremely dangerous work.

Crocodiles lose and regrow their teeth throughout their lives.

pieces of meat out of his leg, and gashes, mate, just pumping out blood. He's turned on the fence and when I looked up, he was ready to jump straight back in . . . to save my life.[10]

Steve, too, has been injured during the filming of his shows, but none so serious as Wes's terrible encounter. When Steve's injuries are fairly serious, the scenes are cut out of the show.

Steve has filmed fifty episodes of *The Crocodile Hunter* and fifty-two episodes of *Croc Files*, which combines bizarre details and scientific facts in stories about animal anatomy, life cycles, and eating and mating habits. In the *Croc Files* episode "Charlie/How to Catch a Crocodile," Charlie the gigantic crocodile attacks the camera and bites a chunk out of it.

Steve's third television series, *The Crocodile Hunter Diaries*, is about the amazing animal adventures behind the scenes at the Australia Zoo. Steve, Terri, and the rest of the staff care for the zoo's five hundred animals and rescue injured animals. Australia Zoo's veterinarians perform incredible operations to save their lives. And every episode includes moments of extreme

Steve sneaks up behind a venomous snake. Every episode of Steve's television show includes such moments of extreme danger.

danger, such as raiding the nests of female crocodiles or the world's biggest and most-venomous snakes.

The Message

Some fans tune in just to see Steve get bloody from different animal attacks. But most fans are drawn to him because of his passion for the animals, his enthusiasm when hunting them, and his tender devotion to protecting them. Steve says:

> I believe that education is all about being excited about something. Seeing passion and enthusiasm helps push an educational message. That's the main aim in our entire lives is to promote education about wildlife and wilderness areas, save habitats, save endangered species, etc. So, if we can get people excited about animals, then by crikey, it makes it a heck of a lot easier to save them.[11]

CHAPTER FOUR

Wild Future

For Steve Irwin, wrestling crocodiles, collecting poisonous snakes, making television documentaries, and helping to save endangered animals are all part of daily life. And he uses his love of animals to promote a message of conservation worldwide. Steve is an avid guardian of wildlife, and he and Terri devote their lives to saving wildlife habitat. Steve says, "We're into conservation. That's our passion. That's my whole aim in life."[12]

To show their passion, Steve and Terri use money from *The Crocodile Hunter* series to fund special projects such as the Wildlife Protection Association of Australia Inc. In addition, Steve's Endangered Species Unit provides protected habitats for many endangered animals in crisis, such as the koala. And his Australia Zoo offers twenty-four-hour veterinary care to any hurt or endangered animal.

Animals of Australia

Dingo

Kookaburra

Red Kangaroo

Great Barrier Reef

Darwin

Arnhem Land

Kimberley

Indian Ocean

Great Sandy Desert

NORTHERN TERRITORY

Pacific Ocean

QUEENSLAND

Uluru (Ayers Rock)

WESTERN AUSTRALIA

SOUTH AUSTRALIA

Great Dividing Range

Nullarbor Plain

Perth

NEW SOUTH WALES

Byron Bay

Sydney

Canberra

AUSTRALIAN CAPITAL TERRITORY

Southern Ocean

VICTORIA

Melbourne

Tasman Sea

TASMANIA

Emu

Tasmanian Devil

Koala

To conserve and preserve the animals of Australia, like those shown here, Steve and Terri fund special projects like the Wildlife Protection Association of Australia Inc.

Steve spent his whole life helping to create the zoo and care for the animals. But some of the animals, such as crocodiles and turtles, live longer than humans do. Steve and Terri wanted to have a child to pass along the knowledge of how to care for the future of the animals they loved.

One night at the zoo, Terri wrote,

> We were up most of the night talking about our hopes and dreams for conservation and Australia Zoo. There was no doubt in our minds about the next step to take. Steve and I both grew up with a burning passion for saving wildlife. Now we needed to pass on this desire to make a difference in the world. We'd made the big decision. More than anything on Earth, we knew that we wanted a child.[13]

Bindi Sue

On July 24, 1998, the Irwins' first child was born. Much to Terri's surprise, Steve brought the film crew along to film the birth. As soon as their baby girl was born, Steve and Terri named her after two of Steve's favorite animals. Terri said,

> Steve and I had never discussed girls' names much, but as he held our brand-new baby, he sounded certain when he said he wanted to name her Bindi. It was the word **aborigines** use for young girl. It was also the name of one of Steve's favorite crocodiles. "Bindi Sue," I said, thinking of Steve's little dog Sui. Steve immediately took

off to show the entire maternity ward his beautiful Bindi Sue. Never mind that they all had their own new babies, Steve's enthusiasm could not be stifled.[14]

In August 1998, when she was just two weeks old, Bindi traveled to California, where she met her first tarantula. In her first few months, she met all the animals at the zoo. Bindi often travels with her parents, but some places are too dangerous for her, and she and Terri stay home. Terri says she worries about Steve when they are not together: "I don't cope well

Steve Irwin holds up his daughter Bindi above the crowd at the premiere of The Crocodile Hunter: Collision Course, *as his wife Terri looks on.*

Three boys in Timor, Indonesia, wear crocodile hats at a celebration. Steve helped create a safe environment for the crocodiles in Timor.

when I'm not there with him," she says of the dangerous video shoots. "I find it terrifying."[15]

Sacred Crocodiles

One such hazardous place is Timor, a small island in Indonesia that had been divided by war for twenty years. The people who live there believe the crocodile is a sacred animal and that the island is made out of a giant old crocodile. In 1999, after the war, Australian army soldiers saved a huge crocodile named Anthony and a smaller crocodile named Maxine from starvation. They lived in the village of Dili, which had been destroyed by war. Maxine and Anthony lived in filthy cement enclosures and were tortured and sick.

After the war, Steve came to rescue the animals. But Steve's dad taught him to honor the beliefs, traditions, and sacred animals of local people. So instead of taking the crocodiles to his zoo, he created a safe environment in East Timor for the sacred crocodiles. And his zoo raised money to help the people rebuild their sacred traditions, including teaching the children. Steve said,

> We took rubber snakes and squeaky crocodiles, and now all of a sudden the children are finding the little squeaky crocodiles are their fun things. . . . And when we ask, "How do you save a habitat?" maybe the first rule is letting [the local people] have full bellies and healthy children. And then starting to make the animals a cool thing to be proud of instead of something to simply consume or make money out of.[16]

Bindi the Crocodile

Steve enjoys teaching children about wildlife. In 2002 he teamed up with Bindi's favorite band, the Wiggles, to make the *Wiggly Safari* programs for young children. And he also made his first movie that year, the adventure comedy *The Crocodile Hunter: Collision Course*. While shooting the film, Steve proved he has not changed much since he was a child. Between takes he and Bindi wandered off together, and the film crew had to send someone out to look for them. They would often find Steve in the bush showing a dangerous snake to Bindi.

The film crew brought them back to the filming location where Steve captured a crocodile on camera. Some of the filming was pretty scary, especially the part where Steve wrestles underwater with Bindi the crocodile. Steve said,

> There was a lot of blood, my face got caved in by that female croc underwater . . . so that all got [cut out] so that kids could watch it. We had a heck of a job keeping the fear factor down during the main croc capture. Even my own daughter was intimidated by the croc stuff. When we watched it at the premiere a few weeks ago, she ran up and sat on my lap, just to keep in contact because she wasn't sure what was going to happen to me.[17]

Steve gasps for air as he struggles with a crocodile in The Crocodile Hunter: Collision Course. *One of the movie's fight scenes left him with serious injuries.*

Terri, Steve, and Bindi ride an elephant at the Los Angeles premiere of The Crocodile Hunter: Collision Course.

At the **premiere** of the film, the Irwins rode in on an Indonesian elephant and walked down a green carpet lined with snakes and an alligator. But unlike the animals in many Hollywood movies, no one thought of the wild animals in this movie as possible pets. And every penny Steve made from the movie went into wildlife conservation.

Steve has future plans to use money from his films for conservation, saying:

> If our next movie is successful, we'll buy [land in] Indonesia and then we will restore the jungle. If there's some way we can get [an Indonesian citizen] to own a national park in Indonesia where they're not going to log it and it's not going to get burnt out and trashed, then we can return the elephants, whether it be their **offspring** or whatever, to that place.[18]

For the Future

Steve's next project will be *Steve Irwin's Ghosts of War*, a two-part miniseries based on the Pacific conflict of World War II. In *Ghosts of War*, Steve tells battle stories and shows the old guns and bombs that have been left behind in the Pacific region. Steve is also working on a funny cartoon series in which he will lose his arms, legs, and head.

Everything Steve does is about conservation; he says:

> I want to create history. So . . . we're taking the "Croc Hunter" message, we're taking conservation and the greening of our planet to kids' toys, to shirts—you know, our shirts will be an advertisement of conservation. It's like we're taking it to [a high] degree. In fact, we probably won't stop there either. If there's another medium where we can just get people excited about conservation we'll take it, we'll run with it."[19]

Notes

Chapter One: Wild Child

1. Steve Irwin and Terri Irwin, *The Crocodile Hunter: The Incredible Life and Adventures of Steve and Terri Irwin*. New York: Penguin Putnam, 2001, p. 8.

2. Irwin and Irwin, *The Crocodile Hunter*, p. 38.

Chapter Two: Fear and Love

3. Quoted in Sarah Simpson, "Everyone's Favorite Crocodile Wrestler Goes to the Mat for Animals," *Scientific American*, March 26, 2001. www.sciam.com.

4. Irwin and Irwin, *The Crocodile Hunter*, p. 63.

5. Steve Irwin, "The Crocodile Hunter—Frequently Asked Questions," The Official Website of the Crocodile Hunter. www.crocodilehunter.com.

6. Quoted in Larry King interview, "'The Crocodile Hunter' Goes Wild," *Larry King Live*, June 13, 2001. http://web6.infotrac.galegroup.com.

Chapter Three: The Crocodile Hunter

7. Quoted in King interview, "'The Crocodile Hunter' Goes Wild."

8. Quoted in Sandra Lee, "Wild Thing," *USA Weekend Magazine*, June 18, 2000. www.usaweekend.com.

9. Quoted in Lee, "Wild Thing."

10. Quoted in King interview, "'The Crocodile Hunter' Goes Wild."

11. Quoted in Simpson, "Everyone's Favorite Crocodile Wrestler."

Chapter Four: Wild Future

12. Quoted in Steve Dougherty and Shelley Gare, *People Weekly*, "The Bite Stuff: TV's Crocodile Hunter, Steve Irwin, Faces Tooth and Fang with No Worries," October 16, 2000. http://web6.infotrac.galegroup.com.

13. Irwin and Irwin, *The Crocodile Hunter*, p. 171.

14. Irwin and Irwin, *The Crocodile Hunter*, pp. 176–77.

15. Quoted in *People Weekly*, "The Bite Stuff."

16. Quoted in Simpson, "Everyone's Favorite Crocodile Wrestler."

17. Quoted in Anwar Brett, "The Crocodile Hunter: Collision Course," BBC Website, May 15, 2003, www.bbc.co.uk.

18. Quoted in The Movie Chicks Website, "Interview with Steve and Terri Irwin, The Crocodile Hunter: Collision Course," June 21, 2002. www.themoviechicks.com.

19. Quoted in Simpson, "Everyone's Favorite Crocodile Wrestler."

GLOSSARY

aborigine: One of the original or earliest known people of a region.

habitat: The environment where a person, animal, or living community is normally found.

offspring: The children and grandchildren, and other descendants of a person, animal, or plant.

outback: The remote, rural area of a country, especially in Australia or New Zealand.

premiere: The first to take place.

reptile: Cold-blooded, usually egg-laying animals covered with scales or horny plates, such as snakes, lizards, crocodiles, turtles, and dinosaurs.

venomous: Full of poison, usually carried in a bite or sting.

For Further Exploration

Book

Steve Irwin and Terri Irwin, *The Crocodile Hunter: The Incredible Life and Adventures of Steve and Terri Irwin.* New York: Penguin Putnam, 2001. A book written by Steve and Terri about their lives, adventures, and daughter Bindi.

Websites

"The Crocodile Hunter," Animal Planet (http://animal.discovery.com). A website that includes Croc Fan Central, Close Call Clips, photos, FAQ, Talk About Steve, and diaries about the TV shows.

EXN.ca, Crocodile Hunter (www.exn.ca/Crocodile Hunter). Canada's Discovery Channel Croc Hunter site includes articles and video, interactive tours, program details, a fan forum, games, contests, and a best-of video reel.

Official Website of the Crocodile Hunter (www. crocodilehunter.com). A website that includes short biographies of Steve and Terri, FAQs, press clips, Steve's travel diary, Australia Zoo, conservation projects, and snapshots.

Movie

The Crocodile Hunter: Collision Course, prod. and dir. John Stainton, MGM Home Entertainment, 2002. A video starring Steve and Terri Irwin. Steve tries to save a huge crocodile from poachers, but the big croc has swallowed a top-secret U.S. satellite beacon, making them both targets of the U.S. special agents trying to find the beacon.

INDEX

PICTURE CREDITS

Cover Photo: Getty Images
COREL Corporation, 10, 28, 32 (animal images, excluding bottom, center)
© Peter Johnson/CORBIS, 8
Chris Jouan, 32
The Kobal Collection, 19, 24, 37
Landov, 18, 34, 35, 38
PhotoDisc, 32 (bottom, center)
Photofest, 5, 7, 12, 14, 16, 22, 27, 29

ABOUT THE AUTHORS

P.M. Boekhoff is an author of more than twenty-five nonfiction books for children. She has written about history, science, and the lives of creative people. In addition, Boekhoff is an artist who has created murals and theatrical scenic paintings and has illustrated many book covers. In her spare time, she paints, draws, writes poetry, and studies herbal medicine.

Stuart A. Kallen is the author of more than 150 nonfiction books for children and young adults. He has written extensively about Native Americans and American history. In addition, Kallen has written award-winning children's videos and television scripts. In his spare time, Stuart A. Kallen is a singer/song-writer/guitarist in San Diego, California.